Focus on History

edited by Ray Mitchell and Geoffrey Middleton

Georgian England

J. R. C. Yglesias

On the farm

The picture on the opposite page shows a farmhouse and farmyard in Britain, almost two hundred years ago. It tells us about life and work on a farm in Georgian times. The four Georges reigned from 1714–1830.

The farmer's family is busy at work. His wife is feeding her poultry. One of his daughters is milking a cow. There were no milking machines in those days. She had to do it by hand.

The other daughter is crossing the farmyard. Where is she going? Why does she carry a wooden yoke across her shoulders, with empty buckets hanging from each end?

One son is feeding the pigs, and his younger brother is watering the horse. The farmer used his horse for several jobs – for ploughing, for carting and for riding to market. Can you find the wagon in the barn by the haystack?

Now look at the farmhouse. Its roof is made of the same kind of material as the roof of the barn. What are they made from? What do we call this kind of roof?

Where are the dovecotes and the beehives? Where did the farmer and his family get their drinking water? What are some of the jobs that had to be done? What kind of food would the farmer and his family eat?

The picture on this page shows people working on another farm. Find out what each person is doing.

Two hundred years ago some villages still followed the 'open fields' methods of farming. Their way of farming had not changed much for centuries. They still grew their crops in large fields which were divided into strips, and the villagers owned or rented strips of land in each of the village fields.

Notice:

the strips of land shown in the picture

that these open fields have no fences or hedges. Find the narrow grass banks which divide the strips.

Most farmers' strips were scattered all over the various fields. Walking round to look after each particular strip wasted time. Mr. Moxan of Cawthorne (Yorkshire) wrote:

I have 87 strips in the fields nearly two miles (3·2 km) from home. I spend too much time running around the parish instead of farming my land.

The farmers also had to decide as a group the best time for planting and sowing. So, as long as everyone in the village had to cultivate the fields in the same way, there was little chance for any farmer to do what he wanted to improve his fields, crops or cattle, or to farm in his own way.

The old three-year pattern of crop-planting was still in general use when George I came to the throne in 1714. Fields were planted with crops in rotation, like this:

	First year	Second year	Third year
Field A	Wheat	Barley, Oats or Peas and Beans	Fallow (left to rest)
Field B	Barley, Oats or Peas and Beans	Fallow (left to rest)	Wheat
Field C	Fallow (left to rest)	Wheat	Barley, Oats or Peas and Beans

But changes were already taking place. Look at this picture.

Can you see the ridges and furrows — the old strips? Notice that the grassy banks dividing the strips have gone. Hedges and ditches, or fences have been put round the old open fields. The fields are now 'enclosed'.

When this happened the pattern changed: the three-field rotation and the patchwork of strips disappeared. Larger fenced areas made for better cultivation. Wealthy landowners also wanted pasture fields for sheep and cattle.

This enclosure map of Dinnington in Yorkshire was found in a cottage under the foot of a grandfather clock where it acted as a support.

Find the fields where Robert Athorpe and the Duke of Leeds exchanged lands, to make a more compact field which could be enclosed with a hedge or fence.

In the second half of the eighteenth century wealthy landowners and farmers bought up large areas of land and enclosed them. With these new fields, they could develop better crop rotations, new methods of draining land and cultivation.

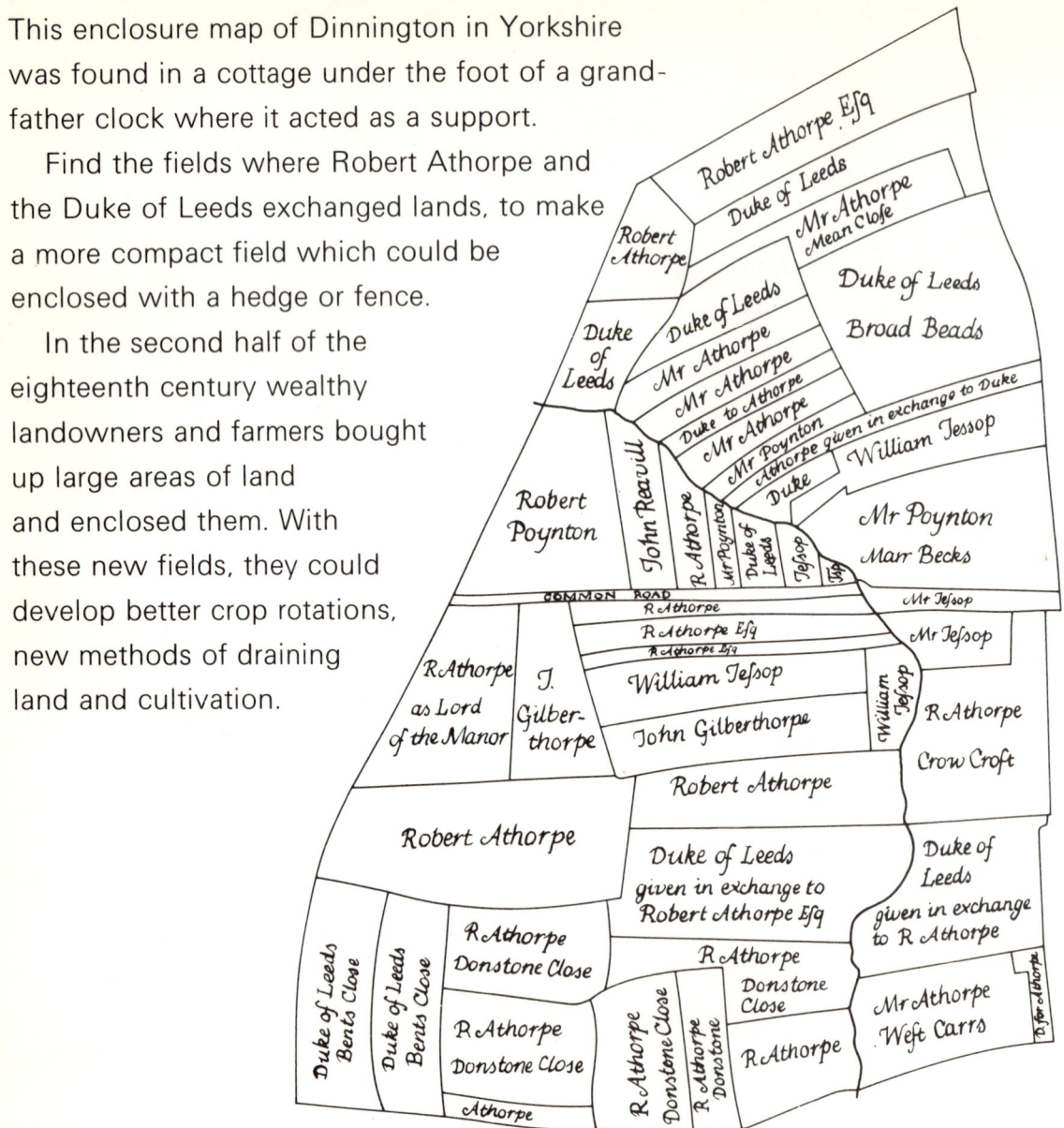

As Robert Hale put it:

'Enclosure gives a liberty of making whatsoever alteration and improvement he (the landowner) shall choose. He may plant and sow what he pleases and in what manner he pleases. Which he cannot do while it lies open.'

New farming methods meant more food. And more food was needed desperately because the population was growing fast.

On the other hand, poor farmers and villagers suffered. They had to sell out or lose their strips, and they lost their grazing rights too.

Each dot on this map represents the enclosure of 1000 acres by Act of Parliament.

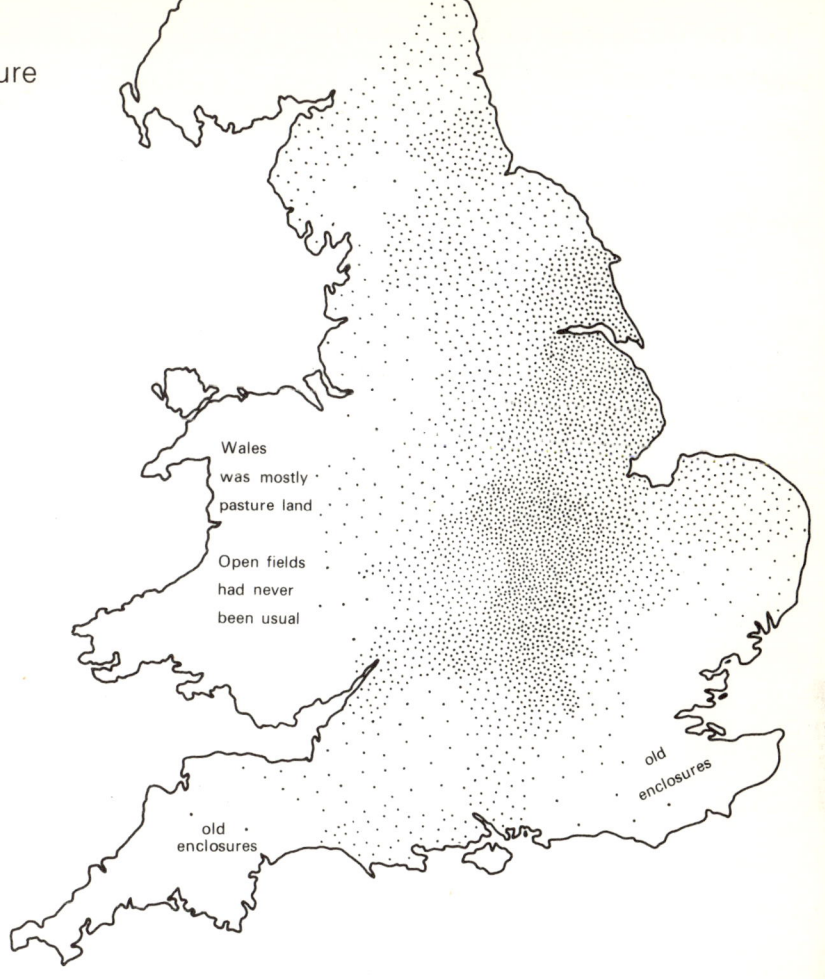

Wales was mostly pasture land

Open fields had never been usual

old enclosures

old enclosures

In which area of Britain was there the greatest number of enclosures: North, South, East, West, Midlands, Scotland or Wales?

Imagine you are a wealthy landowner. Give three reasons why you want to enclose your fields.

Today some farmers are removing the hedges and fences round their fields. Why are they doing this?

Make a model of a farmhouse and farmyard in England 200 years ago. The picture on page 2 will help you.

Cut out figures of the farm-workers at work e.g. the dairy maid carrying a yoke with two buckets of milk.

Draw two diagrams to show the difference between open and enclosed fields, with notes explaining the changes, the advantages and disadvantages. Make an imaginary enclosure map like that on page 6, showing plots and names of farmers, and the exchange of plots.

There were other changes, as we can see if we compare these two ploughs:

The first is a medieval plough which had been used for many years. It was made of wood and was pulled by oxen. Find the yoke harness on the neck of the oxen.

But by 1750 a cast-iron plough had been made.

The mould-board of this plough turned the soil right over. This was a great improvement on the medieval plough.

In both illustrations, find the cutting blade, called the coulter.

Make a model of the second plough and label the coulter and the mould-board.

Draw a picture of farmers ploughing a field using a cast-iron plough.

By the middle of the eighteenth century, too, many more farmers were using horses and this speeded their work.

Now look at these two pictures of seed sowing. The first shows how seed had been sown for hundreds of years. How was the seed carried? How was it sown? If you wanted to sow the seed only in the furrows, why was this scattering by handfuls wasteful?

Now compare this old-fashioned method of sowing seed 'broadcast' by hand, with the modern method which came in after 1745. Look at the splendid four-wheel drill below. Why was this method faster and more accurate? Find the small wooden hopper which carried the seeds and dropped them into the ground. The large hopper was used for manure.

Another model was invented by Jethro Tull and was widely used in this century.

This four Wheel Drill Plow, with a Seed and a Manure Hopper, was first Invented in the Year 1745. and is now in Use with Wm Ellis at Little Gaddesden near Hempstead in Hertfordshire, where any person may View the same. It is so light that a Man may Draw it, but Generally drawn by a pony or little Horse.

When the spring ploughing and sowing was over
everyone joined in haymaking at midsummer.

From the picture of the midday break at haymaking
time name what was used for:
– collecting the hay into heaps,
– lifting the hay from the ground,
– transporting the hay from the field.

Describe the clothes worn by the women. What food
is the woman sitting in the front cutting with her knife?

After the haymaking came sheep washing
and sheep shearing in July, followed by
the best season of all – harvest time.

Draw a picture to show some of the merrymaking at haymaking. Give it a
title and name the month of the year. Does your school or church have a
harvest festival in September? Describe it.

In September harvest time was in full swing. There would be plenty of home-brewed ale, plenty of fruit and honey and all sorts of feasts with dancing on the village green.

Describe the clothes worn by the men cutting the wheat in this picture. What is the difference between their headgear? Point out which man is binding up a handful of wheat after it has been cut with a sickle. How many sickles are shown in this picture? What has caught the attention of the man standing up?

Is it true to say that harvesting was a back-breaking job in those days? Today farmers use a combine harvester. What jobs does this machine 'combine'?

Look at this flail being used for threshing the corn in the barn. Leather joined together the two pieces of wood. Threshing by hand still took a long time.

Draw a picture of an eighteenth century cart loaded with bundles of wheat on its way to the village barn for threshing (separating the grain from the corn by beating).

Find each of these items among the pictures shown in the first ten pages of this book:

sickles – hay rake – horse and cart – yoked oxen – coulter on a cast-iron plough – a seed drilling machine.

In this picture, a farmer is giving orders to a farm labourer. You can tell which man is the farmer by his clothes. What is he wearing? What two farm tools are shown here? What else is shown?

New estate owners built roads, improved drainage, and used new machinery. Some grew better crops by altering the order of rotation. They followed Viscount Townshend, of Norfolk, and started to grow turnips and clover. This gave winter food for their cattle and meant that they could plan a four-crop rotation, so land was not left fallow every third year.

Other men like Robert Bakewell, of Dishley in Leicestershire, and Thomas Coke, of Holkham in Norfolk, introduced new and better breeds of sheep and cattle. This gave more food for the increasing population, for these cattle were bred specially to give more meat.

You can see the improvement from these records, showing average weights of animals, at Smithfield Market in London.

	1700	1800
Black Cattle	370 lb	800 lb
Sheep	28 lb	80 lb
Calves	50 lb	148 lb
Lambs	18 lb	50 lb

Thomas Coke also invited farmers to his annual sheep shearings, where they could see and discuss the new types of farming. This was the beginning of our famous Agricultural Shows.

Find out more about Coke's annual sheep shearings and the first Agricultural Shows. Is an annual Show held in your county? Where is it held and what can you see there?

Below is a picture called 'Harvest Home'. It shows the merrymaking at the end of harvest. Look for:
— the farmer,
— the musicians.
— the dancers. What else can you find?

Village life

Arthur Young travelled all over England at this time and he wrote about what he saw. He noted much that was good, much that was bad. He recognised that in spite of enclosure special skills were still needed: blacksmiths, bakers, cordwainers (shoemakers), victuallers (grocers) and others could still make a living in the village.

The poet John Clare was perhaps more fortunate than those who lived in a one-room house without glass windows, and only mud and straw walls. Here is a picture of his cottage at Helpston.

Notice the roof of Clare's cottage. Compare it with those in this picture of a village green near Romford, Essex. Have any other houses got dormer windows in the roof like Clare's?

Find the shop and the different kinds of transport.

Can you see the blind beggar and the geese?

Look carefully back at the picture at the top of page 13. Can you see Thomas Coke's house in the distance? It is a large mansion compared with the houses on the village green near Romford shown on page 14. Look also at the farmhouse on page 2. Which of these houses would you choose to live in if you had been alive in the eighteenth century? Make a model of the one you choose.

People like Coke, who lived in large mansions, could afford luxuries like wax candles, private carriages and horses, lovely gardens, coal fires and visits to London.

But the villagers' life was hard. They toiled and starved, sometimes they rioted and burned hayricks. They tried to avoid the drift to factory work in the new towns springing up all over the Midlands and North.

This picture shows a cottage in Yorkshire. What are the mother, grand-mother and daughter doing? Notice the basket grate and the huge chimney. There is no staircase, only a ladder to reach the upstairs room. What sort of windows are there in this cottage?

Make a model of a huge cottage fireplace. Why might a cottage family have to burn peat or cow dung instead of wood at the end of the eighteenth century?

The labourer's family would all get up at dawn and go to bed at sunset. They made tallow candles from melted mutton fat, and rushlights were made by dipping peeled sticks in hot tallow.

Here are an iron candlestick, a rushlight holder and a lantern with horn windows. Which of these is which?

Make a model of an 18th century village street and green. Include thatched cottages with dormer windows — a shop — a horse and wagon — some animals on the green — and a pond. Construct a simple cottage table and on it put examples of the sort of food and utensils used in the eighteenth century.

Make a picture frieze called: A day in the life of a poor village labourer in the eighteenth century.

Show the family at breakfast — then the labourer at work in the fields — his family at work at home — then the evening meal — and finally the family asleep on the floor. Write notes about each picture and paste them underneath the wall frieze.

Make a model in a large cardboard box of the interior of an eighteenth century cottage. Make some simple furniture from balsa wood and cut out cardboard figures of women spinning and weaving inside the cottage.

You will find tools used by farmers in the eighteenth century in some museums. Visit any near where you live or when on holiday. Make drawings and write notes of what you find there.

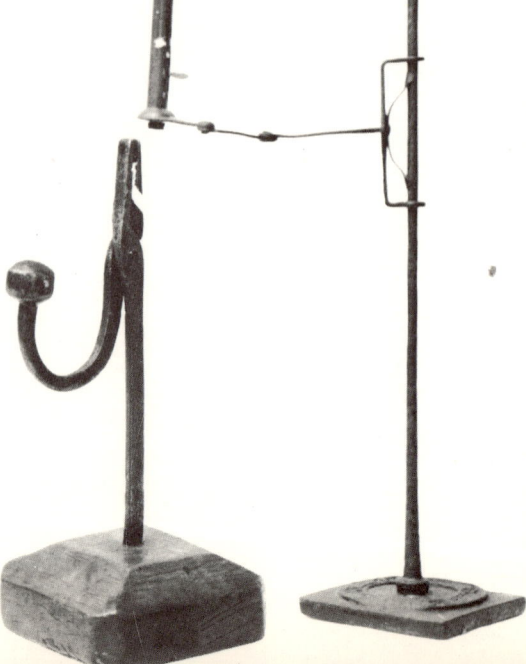

William Cobbett was another traveller, who recorded his journeys and opinions in his famous book *Rural Rides.*

This is what he wrote about the life of labourers after enclosure:

The labourers' houses are beggarly in the extreme. The men and boys have dirty faces and dirty smock coats and shirts. Every inch of land is taken over by the rich, and the wretched labourer has not a stick of wood and no place for a pig or cow to graze.

Cobbett remembers staying in his grandmother's little cottage. For breakfast they had bread and milk; for dinner apple-pudding; and for supper, bread and cheese.

In the farmhouse food would be better and more varied. They would even have knives and forks like the well-to-do landowners, squires and parsons.

Below you can see some of the tableware of those days. These examples can be seen today in a museum at Leicester, but your own museum may have collections too. If so, make drawings and write notes about what you find there.

There was of course the occasional rabbit to be caught in the woods and
sometimes fish from the local streams. Those who had some land round
their cottage could grow vegetables, and others might keep poultry or a pig
or two. Three acres would be enough for a cow. Much less was needed for a
vegetable garden.

Before enclosure pigs could get fat from eating acorns in the woods.
In the autumn each year there would be a great pig-killing day in the village
and huge slices of pork were pickled in wooden tubs. Slices of bacon would
be smoked by hanging them over the fire.

Working on the land in those days meant getting up at six in the morning
to go out in the fields. Then about ten o'clock in the morning most people
would go back to their cottages where they sat on stools and ate their dinner.
On Fridays most people would eat fish — often pickled herrings or mussels
and cockles. After more work in the fields supper would be taken at about
four o'clock.

When a poor family went to bed they slept on the floor on straw mattresses
covered with blankets for warmth and perhaps a log for a pillow.

Many country people could
not afford to bake their own
bread because of the cost of
fuel, so they took their bread
to the baker's oven in the
village and paid him to bake it
for them. The bread was
usually made from wheat flour.

The people inside this cottage — in Scotland — are rather better off than the Yorkshire family shown in page 15. Compare the two scenes.

Find the box-bed and the chickens sharing the living space. Where do the chickens roost?

How do the cooking conditions vary?

What is the boy beside the fire doing?

Can you see the hams for curing? What else is hanging on the same beam?

Find the lantern. Has it a horn window like the one on page 16?

Where are the plates and dishes kept?

Describe the clothes worn by the women and by the man sitting in the chair. What kind of pipe is he smoking?

What are the young ladies doing?

But most cottagers at least got two good meals a year. In Spring and Autumn landlord and parson gave a party for the village. You can see one of these occasions above.

How can you tell that the villagers are enjoying themselves? Point at some who have had more than enough to eat and drink.

They have finished the roast beef, chicken, pigeon pie, fruit tart, cakes and plum pudding. They started at 11 o'clock. What is the time now? Find the overturned mug of ale.

Parson Woodforde of Weston Langville in Norfolk was always generous to the poor — especially at Christmas. At the same time he bought tea from smugglers, watched executions and bear baiting and didn't bother whether people came to Church or not.

But parsons were not always popular. They were often disliked because one-tenth (a tithe) of all farm produce had to be given to the Church.

Half the villages of England had no parson anyhow.

In some places there were village schools and the parson was often the village school master as well.

This is a picture of a parson's school in 1730. Look carefully at the picture and discover two subjects taught in the school. How is the parson dressed? Notice that he keeps his hat on. Did the boys come to school in hats?

Look at the picture of the charity school below.

Point out any differences in the clothes of this schoolmaster and the parson shown in the first picture. Can you see the slates hanging underneath the benches?

Write either an account in your diary for Sept 29. 1780 (Michaelmas Day) called the Parish Dinner, or The First Day I went to Parson's School.

Amusements and games

Of course local squires, landowners and even parsons lived comfortably enough. They had time and money for foxhunting — the great sport of the century.

Describe the scene above. Where is the meeting in this picture? Describe the huntsmen's clothes.

Find out some facts about foxhunting today. What clothes do huntsmen wear; where do they meet?

The rich also enjoyed partridge-shooting and race-meetings.

This is a picture of the famous Derby Sweepstakes race at Epsom in 1791. Make a list of all that you can see.

Rich and poor in those days enjoyed bull-baiting and cockfighting.

The bull is tied by the horns to a bull-ring on the ground. Can you see the dogs worrying it? What has happened to the dogs here? Pick out rich and poor spectators. What else can you find?

Below you can see a picture of a cockfight. People gambled as to which cock would win. The cocks wore spurs for attacking and killing each other. Can you find:
– the deaf old man? What is he using for a hearing aid?
– the man who has just thrown a coin into the ring?
– the men taking snuff? What is snuff?

Cricket was less violent. Here is a game in London in 1743.

Describe the bat and the stumps. What sort of clothes were worn? Find the scorer. Here are some of the rules of the London Cricket Club:

'Laws for ye Bowlers 4 Balls an Over
Ye Bowlers must deliver Ye Ball with one foot behind ye Crease even with ye Wicket, and when he has bowled one ball or more shall bowl to ye number of 4 before he changes Wickets, and he shall change but once in ye same Innings.'

The ladies in the picture on the right are playing ninepins, another popular game of the period.

Maypole dancing

Football was pretty violent. A game could take all day. The number of players was unlimited. There were no rules. The goals might be three miles apart. As someone wrote at the time:

'There were all kinds of foul play even beastly fury, murder and extreme violence.'

Dancing round the maypole and morris dancing were less dangerous! Quiet sports and games included:

bowls noggs (or ninepins), shove-board, trippet (knur and spell), backgammon.

Find out some facts about some of these quieter games and dances. (knur and spell is known in the West Riding today).

In spite of all these sports and games, violent and not so violent, the locals often caused complaints like this:

'Many did come and disguise themselves some putting on women's apparell and other longe haire and beardes and arminge themselves went upp and down with shott of guns.'

A game of bowls in a Suffolk village

Paint large pictures of bull-baiting, cock-fighting, cricket and bowls in the eighteenth century.

Make a book called Fun and Games in the Eighteenth Century. Include a page on each of the following: bull-baiting — cock-fighting — cricket — football — dancing round the maypole — morris dancing — bowls — hunting — shooting and fishing. Books in your school or local library will give you more information.

Look again at the pictures of cock-fighting and bull-baiting and of the dancing bear below. Find the dogs and the monkey. Write all you can about the way in which animals were sometimes treated in the eighteenth century.

A dancing bear

Country life – wealthy wives and daughters

Country life was not all hunting, shooting and fishing. Wives and daughters of the wealthy landowners had more time on their hands. Oliver Goldsmith has given us this scene in his book *The Vicar of Wakefield*.

'We were generally awakened in the morning by music, and on fine days rode a-hunting. The hours between breakfast and dinner the ladies devoted to dress and study; they usually read a page, and then gazed at themselves in the glass . . .

'At dinner my wife took the lead; for, as she always insisted on carving everything herself, it being her mother's way, she gave us, upon these occasions, the history of every dish.

'When we had dined, to prevent the ladies leaving us, I generally ordered the table to be removed; and sometimes, with the music master's assistance, the girls would give us a very agreeable concert.

'Walking out, drinking tea, country dances, and forfeits, shortened the rest of the day, without the assistance of cards, as I hated all manner of gaming.'

Describe the aristocratic scene shown in this picture – the musical instruments, the clothes, the hairstyles, the decorations, the chairs.

Not everyone enjoyed country life. Lady Louisa Bute (a prime minister's daughter) was bored living in the country — at Luton Hoo. 'It was a dull place for young people' she wrote, 'trailing to the farm and dawdling to the flower garden.' But if she wore her hair like the lady with the grapes in this picture, she must have been kept busy!

Luton Hoo: The country home of Lady Louisa Bute

Here is the dining-room at Luton Hoo. Look carefully at:
— the candelabra with candles,
— the large dining-table,
— the silver dishes on the serving table,
— the tapestries on the walls.

The next picture shows a room designed about 1756 for the Duke of Norfolk, in Norfolk House, St. James's Square, London, Notice:
— his coronet and monogram over the door,
— the decoration on the walls and ceiling,
— the large mirror over the fireplace,
— the writing table, chairs and stool.
  (This house was pulled down in 1938.)

This is a bedroom of a villa by the River Thames at Hampton. The villa belonged to David Garrick, the famous actor. All the furniture was painted — Can you see the Chinese patterns? The wardrobe has mirrors on the doors. What special name is given to this type of bed?

Look at the lower picture of a kitchen in a large house. How many fireplaces are there?

What food can you see:
— hanging on the wall,
— being weighed,
— on the floor, waiting to be cooked?

Here is a rich family at tea, in a large town or country house, about 1771.

Can you see that the tea cups — like the coffee bowls on page 48 — have no handles? Point out the teapot and sugar basin. The tall pot (urn) is for hot water. What toy has one of the little girls got? Describe the clothes and hair styles.

Mealtimes varied. But in wealthy society we have an eyewitness account from the French Duc de Lioncourt who wrote:

'Throughout England it is the custom to breakfast together, the meal resembling a dinner or supper in France. The commonest breakfast hour is 9 o'clock and by that time the ladies are fully dressed with their hair properly done for the day. Breakfast consists of tea and bread and butter in various forms. In the houses of the rich you have coffee, chocolate and so on. The morning newspapers are on the table and those who want to do so read them during breakfast, so that the conversation is not of a lively nature.

'At 10 o'clock or 10.30 each member of the party goes off on his own — hunting, fishing or walking. So the day passes till 4 o'clock, but at 4 o'clock precisely you must present yourself in the drawing room with a great deal more ceremony than we are accustomed to in France. This sudden change of social manners is quite astonishing and I was deeply struck by it. In the morning you come down in riding boots and a shabby coat, you sit where you like, you behave exactly as if you were all by yourself, no one takes any notice of you, and it is all extremely comfortable. But in the evening, unless you have just arrived, you must be well-washed and well-groomed.'

Look carefully at the beautiful wine-glasses and candlestick used by people in large houses at this time. Find more glasses and other tableware in museums and in any large historical houses open to the public. Draw them.

London life

Lady Louisa Bute lived in the country at Luton Hoo, which you saw on page 28. Two famous architects, Robert Adam and his brother James, designed Luton Hoo and many other houses.

Louisa would have preferred one of the Adam houses in Adelphi Terrace. This famous London street was completed in the eighteenth century and pulled down in the 1930s.

Notice the elegant iron railings in this street.

From this picture you can see how Lady Louisa Bute might have travelled from Luton to London. Why would torches be unnecessary in this street?

Look carefully at the entrances of Luton Hoo on page 28 and this entrance porch of Chandos House in London, also designed by the Adams. What have they in common?

Find out all you can about the Adam brothers and any other famous architects who lived at that time.

This is a picture painted by a famous Venetian artist known as Canaletto.
It shows the River Thames flowing through London. At this time the river
was still used as a busy street.

Find Wren's St. Paul's Cathedral. There were many other churches in the
city of London at that time. How has the artist shown this?

Describe the costume of the fine ladies and gentlemen on the river terrace.

How many different kinds of boats can you find on the river? What were they being used for?

Can you find the ferry boats taking passengers from one river bank to the other? Find one of the landing stages where people could board and alight from the ferry boats. Describe the costume of the watermen and their passengers.

Above you can see Hyde Park Corner towards the end of the eighteenth
century. Today some 100,000 cars pass this point every twenty-four hours.
The building on the right is St. George's Hospital, still there today.

The driver of the wagon is wearing a smock — he comes from the country.
The milkmaid uses the same harness as the one shown on page 2. What is it
called? How does the street lighting differ from that in Adelphi Terrace shown
on page 33? What other kinds of transport can you find?

The surface of London streets was poor compared with today's roads, but
the streets were not so full of holes and water as were the country roads.

Read this eye-witness account by Daniel Defoe, the author of *Robinson
Crusoe*. This is what he saw in Lewes, Sussex, in 1724:

I saw an ancient lady drawn to church in her coach with six oxen.
Nor was it done in frolic or humour, but mere necessity, the way being so
stiff and deep that no horses could go in it.

But roads improved rapidly as better surfaces were used and engineers like Macadam and Telford set to work on them. Also turnpikes were started, and owners of turnpike trusts were made responsible for road repairs.

Travellers had to pay to use the roads. The money (toll) was collected at the tollgate or turnpike. Look at this picture of the turnpike at Tottenham Court Road. The charges were listed on a board. Only soldiers, pedestrians (travellers on foot) and Royal Mail coaches went through the turnpike (gate) free. Pedestrians — if not too fat — went through the pillars on the right.

Describe the other people, animals and activities in this scene.

Find out if there were ever any tollgates in your district. Turnpikes are still used at entrances to football grounds and elsewhere today. What do we call these now?

You can read more about transport in *The Transport Revolution* by Roger Watson (Focus on History, Longman).

People in the streets

The smart set had their own private coaches. Here is a picture by George Stubbs of a lady and gentleman driving in a phaeton in 1789. Notice the lady's hat. It is quite practical — held on by pins and very fashionable, and much less extreme than the fashions of a few years later, shown below.

Compare the style of this headgear with that worn by the lady above. This style may have been all the rage among the smart set of the 1790s but it didn't last long. These hair styles must have been very awkward too since the sedan chair was the most usual form of taxi for short town journeys. One artist at least made fun of this kind of hair style. The lovely lady is riding in a sedan chair — but with a trap-door roof!

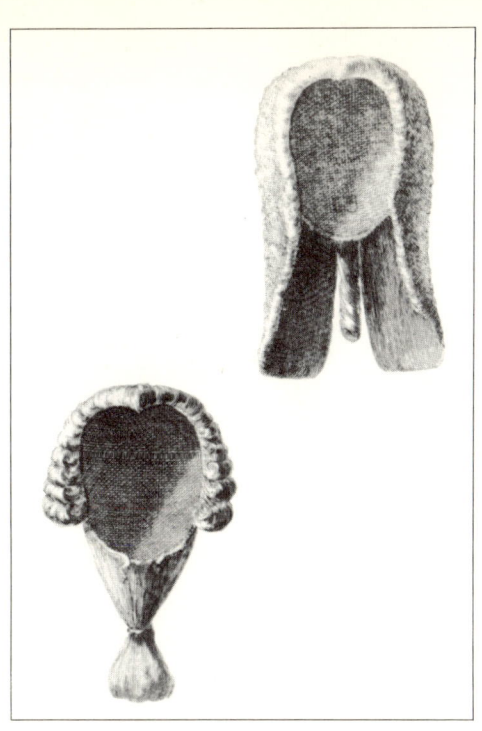

On this page are some styles in clothes and men's wigs, which were seen in the streets of London.

The periwig style is worn by lawyers (barristers) in British courts of law today. Can you find out which one this is?

Wigs were worn brown and black in daytime, but powdered in the evenings. (All servants and workmen wore their own hair shoulder length.)

A man about town might wear a red coat trimmed with braid, blue trousers (breeches style), black hat, black shoes and a lace-fronted shirt with cuffs showing below the cuffs of the coat.

This is what Lord Chesterfield wrote to his son on November 19th 1745:

'The difference between a man of sense and a fop (someone vain and crazy about clothes) is, that the fop values himself upon his dress; and the man of sense laughs at it, at the same time as he knows he must not neglect it.'

Cries of London

Some of the noise in London streets came from horses and carts clattering over cobblestones. Above the shouts of the drivers you would hear the street sellers with their cries: the milkgirl, the apple seller, those 'hawking' or selling brooms, lavender, rosemary, bay, rabbits, hot ginger bread, baskets of cherries, oranges and mackerel. The newsboys, knives and scissors grinders and lamplighters added movement to the busy scene.

Here are some of the street sellers of London.

Find out some eighteenth century cries and listen to some of the songs based on the cries of street sellers.

Are there any street cries in your district today?

Hot spiced gingerbread

Sweet China Oranges

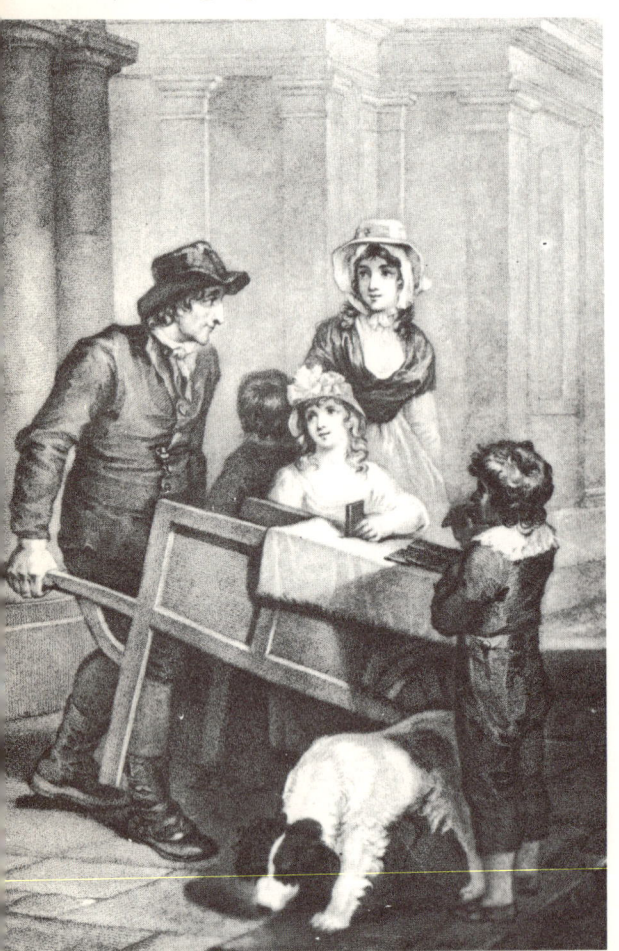

Knives, scissors and razors to grind   *Cherries*

John Gay tells us you could tell the season of the year by watching the street scenes. Here is what he wrote:

'Successive cries the seasons' change declare
And mark the monthly progress of the year.
Hark how the streets with treble voices ring,
To sell the bounteous produce of the spring!
Sweet smelling flowers, and elder's early bud,
With nettle's tender shoots, to cleanse the blood:
And when June's thunder cools the sultry skies
Ev'n Sundays are profaned by mackerel cries.
Walnuts the fruit'rer's hand, in autumn, stain;
Blue plums and juicy pears augment his gain.
When rosemary and bays, the poet's crown,
Are bawl'd in frequent cries through all the town;
Then judge the festival of Christmas near,
Christmas the joyous period of the year.
Now bright holly all your temples stro
With laurel green, and sacred mistletoe.'

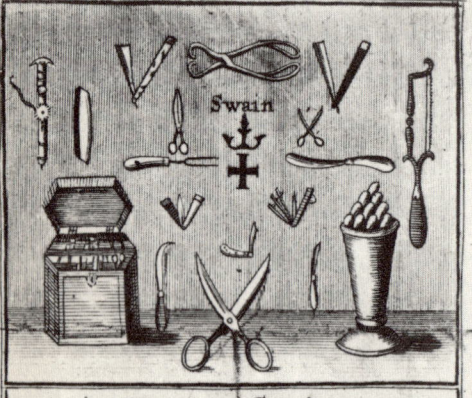

Thomas Swain.
Razor Maker in BEDFORD STREET near Bedford Rowe makes all Sorts of Knives and Forks and Mounts Blades in Silver and Aggat and all other Sorts London

Above is a list of things which were sold at Jones's Warehouse in London.

Read through it carefully and write down those things you would have liked to buy. Are there any which you can still buy today?

Look at the notice on the left issued by Thomas Swain, a razor maker in London. From the picture find what other kinds of instruments he made.

The chemist and his cures

As well as hawkers in the streets there were shops. Here is a reconstruction from the Castle Museum at York.

In the window of the copper shop on the left are saucepans, coffee pots and jugs. There are also jelly moulds, beer mugs and tea urns. Find out what a copper warming pan looked like, what it was used for, and how it was heated.

On the right of the picture is the chemist's shop. (He was called the apothecary.) He helped those too poor to go to a doctor and sold drugs and medicines.

According to one advertisement of the times you could buy a cure for 'coughs, colds, asthma, wheezings and all sorts of consumptions'. As for 'wind and pains in the stomach and bowels' — one box of Mr. Speediman's stomach pills (it was claimed) would 'disperse the wind in a very surprising manner' — and very expensive it was. A box cost almost as much as a working man's weekly wage.

Here are a few cheaper cures:

— for deafness: pour in the ear dripping from a hedgehog;

— for asthma: swallow young frogs;

— for pimples: carry a dried toad in a silk bag round your neck.

Find out why some people today wear a metal bangle round their wrist or arm. Do you know any cheap cures for toothache or earache?

In the eighteenth century most illnesses were treated by 'blood-letting' — your vein was opened up with a knife and a couple of pints of blood were drained off. Or a doctor might use a leech — a slimy, black kind of worm. Leeches stuck to the flesh and sucked your blood, then dropped off when full up. These two doctors have just arrived to see their patient.

There were no painkilling drugs or anaesthetics. Look in the picture on the left at some of the strange creatures the apothecary used for his cures.

THE
APOTHECARY

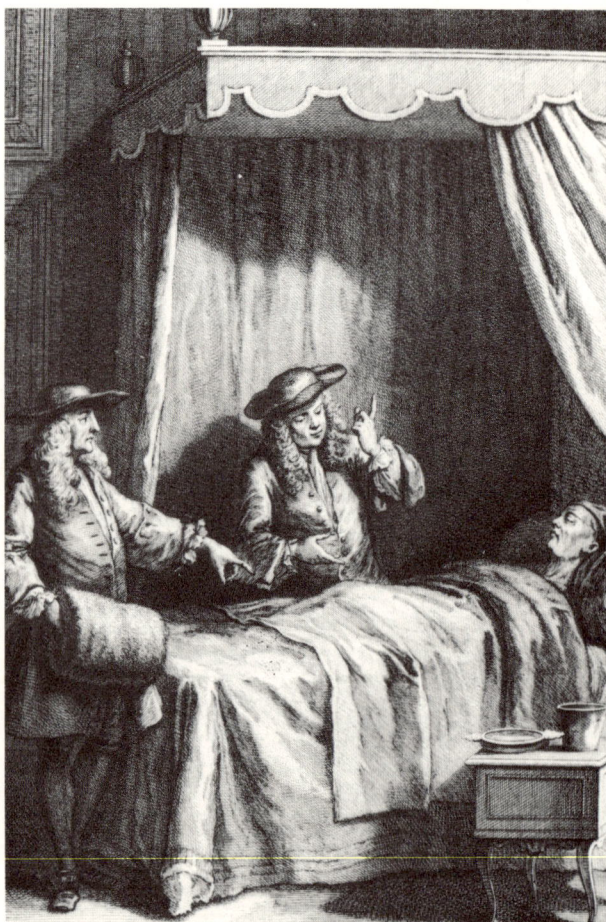

In the country you had to rely more on travelling hawkers because there were fewer shops in the villages. But in London, town and country came together. Look at this picture of Bloomsbury Square — a busy part of London with some town houses of the rich. Even so the setting is quite country-like.

What evidence of country life can you see?

Would you say that the carriage on the left is a phaeton? Compare it with the one on page 38.

Would you call any of the men here 'fops'?

Describe how the men are dressed.

Describe the lady's hat.

Why would you not need a lighted torch to find your way to one of these houses?

Why would Bloomsbury Square be noisy?

Do not think that London was all joy and full only of elegant people living in splendid houses. Many people with sick minds were labelled 'lunatics' and chained up. At one place in London — called Bedlam, you could pay a penny to look at poor wretches in chains, or being thrown in cold baths, or being beaten. But conditions improved slightly after 1770.

Hogarth gave us many true pictures of eighteenth century England. (Look back to page 23.) He was a cartoonist — his drawings were funny, fierce, sad and serious. He drew his pictures to draw attention to the slums and squalor of eighteenth century London, rather as Dickens (100 years later) wrote stories like *Oliver Twist* to draw attention to the slums and squalor of the nineteenth century.

Here is a picture of Bedlam by Hogarth.

Point out the ladies of fashion who are 'penny-visiting'. What is happening to the new arrival on the floor? Describe some of the other lunatics.

Penny-visiting was stopped after 1770 and a better hospital was opened at St. Luke's.

Hogarth drew attention to many other social evils. Here is another of his pictures — called Gin Lane.

Find the shop signs — the pawnbroker's, the gin shop and the coffin maker's. Hogarth shows people crowding into the pawnbroker's to pawn goods for money to buy more gin.

Find:
— the helpless man in the wheelbarrow
— the drunken woman on the steps, allowing her child to fall over the railings.
— the baby having gin poured into its mouth, and
— the blind man and his dog.

There were indeed over 6,000 gin shops and about 7,000,000 gallons were drunk in a year. Hogarth exposed this and other evils, and Parliament limited sales after 1751.

Coffee and tea were also popular drinks, but were less harmful. Men met and gossiped regularly in coffee houses in London.

Notice:
— the coffee pots with their long spouts, being kept warm in front of the fire.
— that the coffee was drunk from bowls without handles and not from cups as we use today.

Dr. Johnson taking tea

What kind of hats, wigs and clothes are the men wearing?

Describe the furniture.

A famous author, Dr. Johnson, liked to meet his friends in a coffee house. He was also, as he said, 'a hardened tea drinker'. Here you see him taking a lump of sugar.

Men kept their hats on most of the time in coffee houses and at the theatre, as you can see above. The picture shows Covent Garden Theatre in 1763.

How is the position of some of the boxes different from those in a modern theatre? Notice that some of the audience are talking to the actors or interrupting them. (They are causing a riot because the theatre managers refused to lower the price of seats.) Some are trying to climb on to the stage. Find the orchestra trying to hide.

Look at this picture of Richard Brindsley Sheridan. He was the manager of Drury Lane Theatre and a brilliant playwright. Notice his powdered wig, his fine linen shirt and velvet-collared coat. Of him Fanny Burney wrote:

'He is tall and very upright, and his appearance and dress are at once manly and fashionable without the smallest tincture (trace) of foppery.'

In this picture find:
— the Punch and Judy show
— the soldier and the sailor with his pipe
— the coach
— the young street sweeper
— the dancers.

Notice the women's frilled bonnets and the men's tall hats, which show that the picture was painted in late Georgian or early Victorian times. Look back at pages 37 and 49 and point out the differences between the clothes shown there and the ones on this page.

If you went to a dance in London you would take part in the 'cotillion' as shown below. In fact, most dances like the cotillion were danced in groups, not in pairs. Look at the picture below: What musical instruments are being used? Describe the shoes worn by the men and the women. What kind of wigs can you see?

Make a model of a London street scene showing shops, street lighting and transport.

Find out all you can about doctors and chemists in the eighteenth century.

Make a picture frieze showing eighteenth century cures and drugs.

Write a short story about either Gin Lane or A Visit to Bedlam.

Make a model of the inside of an eighteenth century coffee house.

Greenwich fair

This is what Voltaire, a French writer, wrote about a visit to Greenwich in 1726:

> 'I halted near Greenwich on the banks of the Thames. This lovely river that never floods and whose banks are green and flowery all the year round was covered for miles with two lines of merchant ships that had spread out their sails in honour of the king and queen who were sailing on the river in a gilded barge.'

Traffic on the River Thames in those days was just as busy as on the London streets — and just as smelly, whatever Voltaire may have written.

Greenwich Palace looks much the same today. But the Thames looks very different even if it does not smell so badly.

Point out what boats might still be seen on the Thames today, and which would not be seen today.

Find out what Greenwich Palace is used for today.

Try to hear some of Handel's Water Music, which was composed for King George III to listen to one summer evening in his gilded barge on the Thames.

There was a great fair at Greenwich on the occasion of Voltaire's visit. One of the things he said was:

'There were two poles: from the top of one hung a great big hat and from the other floated a lady's petticoat. I was agreeably surprised when I was told that it was a girls' race and that, in addition to receiving the purse (a money prize), the winner would be given, as a mark of honour, the petticoat that flew from the top of the pole.'

This picture is much the same scene as the one described at Greenwich. The prize for this, the women's race, is a smock. Where is it hanging? How can you tell that the man reading the notice is probably a rich gentleman? (Refer to his headgear.) What animals are to be seen? Point out a wooden cask of beer — two boys fighting — a woman driver in a hurry — anyone who has had too much to drink — a dovecote — a windmill.

This is how an unknown poet described Greenwich fair:

When merry bells the merry time
Of Holydays declare,
What place for sport and pastime
With Greenwich can compare.

Of Fiddling and of Dancing
When we have had our fill,
We'll take a turn into the Park
And then run down the Hill

The 'Prentices from London
Their Sweethearts hither bring
And some at thread the needle play
While others join the ring.

Make a picture frieze of A Visit to Greenwich Fair showing boats on the
River Thames, Greenwich Palace, the scene at the fair and the petticoat race.

St. Bartholomew fair

Londoners liked going to fairs. A famous one was held at Smithfield for three days in August and was known as St. Bartholomew fair. Here were peep-shows, plays, conjurers, the Big Wheel and various stalls. Find all these in the centre picture of the lady's fan. The other pictures are enlargements and will help you.

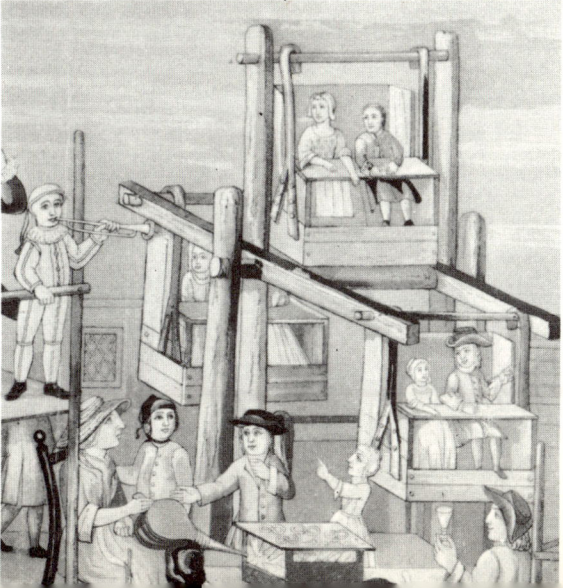

Eating in large houses in London was sometimes rather tiring. Here is a description from the Duc de Lioncourt:

'Dinner is one of the most wearisome of English experiences, lasting, as it does, for four or five hours.

The courses are much the same as in France except that the use of sauce is unknown in the English kitchen. All the dishes consist of various meats either boiled or roasted and of joints weighing about twenty or thirty pounds.

After the sweets, you are given water in small bowls of very clean glass in order to rinse your mouth. This ceremony over, the cloth is removed and you behold the most beautiful table that it is possible to see. It is indeed remarkable that the English are so much given to the use of mahogany; not only are their tables generally made of it, but also their doors and seats and the handrails of their staircases.'

Of course dinner was not finished when the cloth was removed, as the Duc observed:

'The ladies drink a glass or two of wine and at the end of half an hour all go out together. It is then that real enjoyment begins. Everyone has to drink in his turn, for the bottles make a continuous circuit of the table and the host takes note that everyone is drinking in his turn.

'At the end of two or three hours a servant announces that tea is ready and conducts the gentlemen from their drinking to join the ladies in the drawing-room, where they are usually employed in making tea and coffee.'

But down at the Greenwich Workhouse food was not so good. Here is the menu:

Monday	Milk Pottage	Pease Soup	Bread and Cheese
Tuesday	Rice Milk	Salt Fish and Potatoes	Bread and Cheese
Wednesday	Milk Pottage	Pease Soup	Bread and Cheese
Thursday	Rice Milk	Meat, Potatoes, Broth	Bread and Cheese
Friday	Bread and Butter	Suet Pudding	Bread and Cheese
Saturday	Rice Milk	Pease Soup	Bread and Cheese
Sunday	Milk Pottage	Meat, Potatoes, Broth	Bread and Cheese

Allowances:

Bread to adults, one pound; to children, three quarters of a pound, except with respect to the children only, on the day when rice milk is supplied for breakfast, then no more than ten ounces are to be allowed to each.

Beef, half a pound for each person, on every meat day.

Cheese: three ounces, or in lieu (instead), one ounce of butter.

Salt and Fish: one pound, for each person, on every fish day.

Scotch barley is to be boiled in the broth, every meat day and distributed with the broth.

For prisoners conditions were even worse. Below is a picture of John Howard visiting a prison. He tried to reform these terrible conditions. Describe the picture. How can you distinguish John Howard? Find out more about him and his work.

For home cooking there were fewer cookery books than there are today. Even so Mrs. Glasse wrote out quite a few recipes. No doubt you had to be rich to make this one — her idea of a 'plum-pudding for Christmas'.

'Take a leg and shin of beef, put them into eight gallons of water, and boil them till they are very tender, and when the broth is strong, strain it out; wipe the pot and put in the broth again; then slice six penny-loaves thin, cut off the top and bottom, put some of the liquor to it, cover it up and let it stand a quarter of an hour, boil it and strain it, and then put it into your pot; let it boil a quarter of an hour, then put in five pounds of raisins of the sun stoned, and two pounds of prunes, and let them boil till they swell; then put in three-quarters of an ounce of mace, half an ounce of cloves, two nutmegs, all of them beat fine, and mix it with a little liquor cold, and put them in a very little while, and take off the pot, then put in three pounds of sugar, add a little salt, a quart of sack, a quart of claret, and the juice of two or three lemons. You may thicken with sago instead of bread (if you please); pour them into earthen pans and keep them for use.'

Bath in the eighteenth century

An eighteenth century writer, Tobias Smollett, wrote:

'Bath is to me a new world — All is gaiety, good-humour, and diversion. The eye is continually entertained with the splendour of dress and equipage and the ear with the sound of coaches, chaises, chairs and other carriages. The merry bells ring round, from morn till night. We have music in the pump room every morning, cotillions every forenoon in the rooms, balls twice a week, and concerts every other night, besides private assemblies, and parties without number.

As soon as we were settled in lodgings we were visited by the Master of the Ceremonies; a pretty little gentleman, so sweet, so fine, so civil, and polite, that in our country he might pass for the Prince of Wales; then he talks so charmingly, both in verse and prose; that you would be delighted to hear him discourse; for you must know he is a great writer, and has got five tragedies ready for the stage. He did us the favour to dine with us, by my uncle's invitation; and next day squired my aunt and me to every part of Bath, which, to be sure, is an earthly paradise.'

The Master of Ceremonies — Beau Nash

59

Smollett continues:

'The Square, the Circus, and the Parades, put you in mind of the sumptuous palaces represented in prints and pictures; and the new buildings, such as Prince's Row, Harlequin's Row, Bladud's Row and twenty other rows, look like so many enchanted castles, raised on hanging terraces.'

But before considering the life of the rich in eighteenth century Bath look first at the magnificent buildings there.

Above is a picture of Queen Square which was built by John Wood and his son. It is on a slope like so much of Bath.

What sort of carriages are shown? Are the house fronts anything like those in London?

Gay Street leads out of Queen Square up a steep hill to the world-famous Circus, also built by the Woods.

Describe the picture below in detail. Tobias Smollett said the Circus was like the Colosseum in Rome. Find a picture of that and compare them. When was the Colosseum built? Do you agree with Smollett?

Many of John Wood's buildings in Bath were designed to look like ancient Roman temples.

Study the front of the Pump Room above. Notice the triangle at the top of the entrance porch — Roman and Greek temples often had a pediment like that. The Greek words below the pediment mean 'Water is best'.

The pillars, too, are similar to those built by the Greeks and Romans. (The Romans often copied the Greek style.)

Find pictures of Roman temples and buildings and of the Acropolis in Athens where some of the pillars are still standing today. You will see

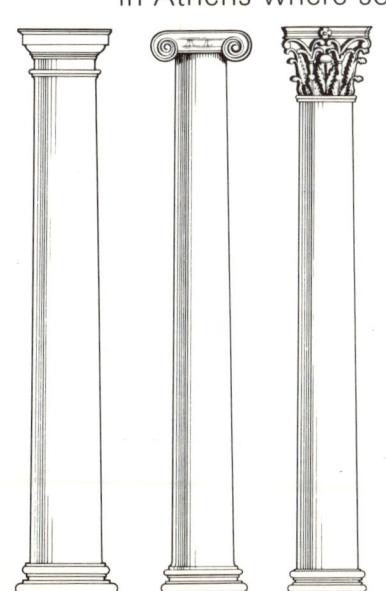

some of them decorated at the top (on the capital) with carved leaves like the Corinthian pillar on the right: on the left are two other pillars with simpler designs on the capital — called Doric and Ionic.

Compare the methods of transport and street lighting with others shown in this book. The three-wheeled chair on the left is called a Bath chair. By the end of the Georgian period gas lighting was being used.

Here is a description of what went on inside the Pump Room at Bath. Again, it is by Tobias Smollett. As you will see from the illustration people went into the bath fully dressed in special clothes.

'At eight in the morning we go in to the Pump Room which is crowded like a Welsh fair; and there you see the highest quality and the lowest trades-folks, jostling each other without ceremony, hail fellow, well met. The noise of the music playing in the gallery, the heat and flavour of such a crowd, and the hum and buzz of their conversation, gave me the headache the first day; but afterwards, all these things became familiar, and even agreeable.

'Right under the Pump Room windows is the King's bath; a huge cistern, where you see the patients up to their necks in hot water. The ladies wear jackets and petticoats of brown linen, with chip hats, in which they fix their handkerchiefs to wipe the sweat from their faces; but, truly, whether it is owing to the steam that surrounds them, or the heat of the water, or the nature of the dress, or to all these causes together, they look so flushed and frightful, that I always turn my eyes another way. My aunt, who says every person of fashion should make her appearance in the bath, as well as in the abbey-church, had a cap with cherry-coloured ribbons to suit her complexion.

'For my part I content myself with drinking about half a pint of water each morning.'

'The pumper, with his wife and servant, attend within a bar; and the glasses of different sizes, stand ranged in order before them, so you have nothing to do but point at that which you choose, and it is filled immediately, hot and sparkling from the pump. It is the only hot water I could ever drink without being sick. Far from having that effect, it is rather agreeable to the taste, grateful to the stomach, and reviving to the spirits.'

COMFORTS of BATH.

Many changes in country and town life took place in Georgian times. Look back through these scenes of life in the Georgian period and compare them with other scenes you have studied.

Index